JEREMY RAISON

Jeremy Raison is an award-winning author of more than 30 stage plays including **The Rain Gathering** (National Theatre, Traverse), **The Sound of My Voice** (Citizens, Assembly, Made In Scotland), **Blitz** (Traverse, Kirkaldy College), **Charlie and the Chocolate Factory** (Sadlers Wells, Dominion West End, National touring, Denmark, Sweden), **Don Juan** (Citizens), **Heart and Soul** (Chester Gateway), **Wake Me In the Morning** (Oran Mor), **Therese Raquin** (Citizens), **Jumping Jack Flash** (Liverpool Everyman), **Savage Britannia** (National Theatre Studio, Mandela), **A Distant Shore** (National Theatre Studio), **Wee Fairy Tales** (Citizens, national touring), **Once Upon A Time** (Chester Gateway) and **A Child of Europe** (Theatre Workshop).

For radio he has written **The Rain Gathering**, **Music To See By**, **The Readers of Broken Wheel Recommend**, **Cuckoo** and **Eavesdropper** (all Radio 4), **Sam's Secret Orchestra** (Radio 3) and a six hour WW1 project for Amazon Audible. For film he wrote and directed **Seen** (BBC1).

Jeremy was Artistic Director of the Glasgow Citizens Theatre for seven years during which time the company tripled its box office, was nominated for seventy three awards and toured internationally, as well as to he West End. He also ran Chester Gateway Theatre for four years winning the TMA/Stage Award for Outstanding Achievement in Regional Theatre.

ALSO BY JEREMY RAISON

The Rain Gathering
Candyland
Bring Me Sunshine
Therese Raquin adapted from Emile Zola
The Sound of My Voice adapted from Ron Butlin
Heart and Soul a play with live soul music

WAKE ME IN THE MORNING

by

Jeremy Raison

I3 PUBLISHING

First published by 13 Publishing in Great Britain, 2014

Wake Me In The Morning copyright © Jeremy Raison 2014

Jeremy Raison has asserted his right to be identified as the author of this work

ISBN 978-1-909809-08-6

A CIP catalogue record for this book is available from the British Library

Cover photograph © Jeremy Raison

For information on the author: www.jeremyraison.com

Wake Me In The Morning was first performed at Oran Mor on 17 February 2014 as part of A Play, A Pie and A Pint. The cast was as follows:

BLONDE	Kirsty McDuff
BULL	Bill Wright
BEACH	Ewan Donald

Director	Liz Carruthers
Designer	Patrick McGurn
Assistant Director	Paul Brotherston

Producers	David MacLennan
	Susannah Armitage
Co-producer	Sarah Macfarlane

CAST

BULL, mid 40s
BEACH, his brother, mid 30s
BLONDE, mid 30s

SET

THE ACTION MOVES BETWEEN A BEDROOM IN
A ONE STOREY HOUSE IN BRENTWOOD, LOS
ANGELES AND AN OFFICE

1. THE BEDROOM

BLONDE'S BEDROOM. SHE'S OVER-DRESSED, MADE UP IMMACULATELY, NERVY, BUT GORGEOUS.

BULL'S IN BLACK TIE. HE'S A STRONG MAN, SELF CONFIDENT, POWERFUL. HE UNLOOSENS HIS TIE, UNDOES THE STUD. HE'S JUST ARRIVED.

BLONDE: The very first time ever I saw you.
BULL: You liked - what you saw.
BLONDE: Yes, sir.

HE MOVES TOWARDS HER.

BULL: Yes, sir -
BLONDE: Why, you're in a mighty big rush, Mr -
BULL: No names.
BLONDE: No?
BULL: People like to listen.
BLONDE: Who's listening?

SHE REALISES HE'S SERIOUS.

BLONDE: Oh boy!

SUDDENLY SHE'S NOT SURE AGAIN.

BLONDE: No, you're teasin' me!
BULL: Now that's one thing I don't expect from you: naïveté.
BLONDE: Maybe I'm still a country girl at heart.
BULL: You think I believe that?

HE MOVES TOWARDS HER AGAIN, SHE HOLDS HIM OFF.

BLONDE: So who would listen? To us. Right now. If I may be so bold as to ask.
BULL: Plenty of folk would like to know what goes on in this room.
BLONDE: Then you're taking a risk. A terrible big, awful risk coming here!
BULL: I'm *not* here.
BLONDE: You're not? Well, you sure coulda fooled me! Oh! I see! "I never saw the man before in my whole life, your worshipful honour, I swear on the bible, so help me God! Especially not in my bedroom. No, sir!"

BULL CHUCKLES AT HER PERFORMANCE.

BLONDE: Just lucky I don't believe in the bible, I guess.
BULL: Smart girl. Now I sure hope we can relax -

BULL TRIES TO GUIDE HER TO THE BED.

BLONDE: You really think I'm smart?
BULL: Smart as a a whip, yes, I do.
BLONDE: My, coming from you, that's – well, that's a mighty fine compliment for a girl, ain't it? Hey, but you sure don't look relaxed, do you? You look awful tense. Like – like – well, I don't know, like that – that fellow with the world crushing his shoulders -
BULL: Atlas.
BLONDE: Well, whaddya know? You're right! Boy, what wouldn't I give to be as clever as your brains!
BULL: You know your way around.

BLONDE: Sure, I can find my way from A to B real quick.
BULL: Now don't you ever think of yourself as stupid.
BLONDE: Who said I was stupid?

HE LOOKS AT HER, WONDERING IF HER
INNOCENCE IS ALL JUST AN ACT.

BLONE: I'm hot. You want to take your jacket off, Mr /
Pr- ?
BULL: Don't.
BLONDE: You want to keep it on?
BULL: We don't use names, I told you.
BLONDE: Oh my. Skullduggery and subterfuge. I feel like
some kind of a spy. Or a – or a terrible criminal!

HE TAKES HIS JACKET OFF.

BULL: So.
BLONDE: So why would a man in your position risk
coming here? Maybe you're like some dog or something that
just can't resist trouble.
BULL: Maybe some trouble's too good to resist.
BLONDE: Which I bet you say to all the girls, don't you?
Only I hope you don't call them trouble too, us girls like to
be treated with a bit more respect, don't we?
BULL: I'll make a note of it. Now I'm sorry to remind you
but we don't have nearly as much time as a beautiful, smart
girl like you so clearly deserves.
BLONDE: Oh, aren't you the snake charmer!
BULL: Trust me, if I could have it any different -
BLONDE: Never trust a man who's alone with a woman,
especially not in a bedroom! Or any room. I sure learned that
a long while back.
BULL: Unfortunately I have a schedule.

BLONDE: You make it sound like you're about to blow your nose or something. That sure don't sound very flattering to a girl, if you'll pardon my French.
BULL: If I'm not in the right place at the right time, people ask questions. You must be busy too –
BLONDE: Except they don't see me.

HE'S NOT SURE WHAT SHE MEANS, BUT BEFORE HE CAN ASK:

BLONDE: So. I'm in your schedule? Wow! Only you're not here, are you? So where are you? Right now!
BULL: I believe I'm attending the dental hygienist.
BLONDE: You must visit him a whole lot! Your teeth are gleaming!
BULL: And I have to leave a whole lot sooner than I would like.
BLONDE: Well, if you don't have the time, maybe you oughta come back when you do.

AN IMPASSE.

BULL: OK, what must I do to make this good for you?
BLONDE: Well, sir, maybe this girl just wants to be treated like a lady. Maybe she wants a little attention -
BULL: You have my full attention, I can assure you.
BLONDE: Whoop-de-doo. The whole free world stops just for silly old me.
BULL: There're plenty of very important people come to my door who get far less.
BLONDE: Oh, baby, poor you!
BULL: This is what was agreed. I'd change it if I could, / you know that –
BLONDE: What did we agree?

BULL: A little fun.

BLONDE: Oh boy, the number of times I heard that in my life. I've had so much fun, I should be the happiest girl in the world, shouldn't I?

BULL: OK,/ maybe it's not the right way -

BLONDE: Hey, don't you think if just one of those guys offered me a little more than fun, I might be different now. Living in some, some different place. With children. A family! A fine old housewife, barefoot in the kitchen -

BULL: Why don't you take off your panties?

THIS STOPS HER IN HER TRACKS. BUT FOR A MOMENT ONLY.

BLONDE: What if I'm not wearing any?

SUDDENLY HE MOVES CLOSE AND PICKS HER UP. HE'S STRONG. HE SEATS HER ON THE BED, KNEELS BETWEEN HER LEGS, STARTS TO UNDO HIS BELT. IT'S GOING TO BE A QUICK FUCK - A QUICK CHECK OF HIS WATCH - HE'S GOING TO GET WHAT HE CAME FOR. HE TAKES HIS HANDS OFF HER TO UNDO HIS TROUSERS, WHEN SHE SURPRISES HIM, PUSHES HIM AWAY, QUICKLY ROLLS OVER THE BED AWAY FROM HIM.

BLONDE: Whoa! Easy, tiger. I might break in half, you're like a big bull in a – in a submarine, aren't you, baby?

BULL: Is this a game? You want me to chase? You need me to dance?

BLONDE: Boy, is that really what you think?

BULL: I'm scheduled to within an inch of my life here.

BLONDE: Well, maybe it's time to change your schedule -

BULL: But that's not really the point here, is it?

BLONDE: No? Then maybe there is no point.
BULL: Wait.

HE REMEMBERS SOMETHING, PRODUCES A BOX FROM HIS JACKET.

BULL: For you.
BLONDE: Boy oh boy! I can't believe you went to all this trouble.

SHE TAKES OUT BEAUTIFUL EARRINGS.

BLONDE: Oh, my - ! You bought these for me? I mean, these must have cost you a pretty penny, that's for sure.

HE MOVES CLOSE BUT SHE STOPS HIM, TO PUT THE EARRINGS ON.

BLONDE: You sure know what a lady likes! Only you didn't chose them, did you? You couldn't have. Not with people watching. Just think of the furore if you bought beautiful earrings and then someone not your wife is seen wearing them!

SHE LOOKS AT THE EARRINGS IN A MIRROR.

BULL: Just relax -

HE MASSAGES HER SHOULDERS.

BLONDE: My. What strong hands you have.
BULL: All the better to hold you with.
BLONDE: And what big white teeth. Wow, I've had men buy me jewels before, but never a Pre -

HE STOPS HER SPEAKING.

BULL: Come on, this is going to have to be quick.

HE TAKES HER BACK TO THE BED, STARTS TO UNDO HIS BELT.

HE'S INTERRUPTED BY KNOCKING.

VOICE (off): Sir.
BULL: Oh, goddamn – damn!
BLONDE: Uh-oh, looks like you're out of time, tiger.
VOICE (off): Sir.

BULL SILENCES HER WITH A SIGN, MOVES CLOSE TO HER. SHE'S NOT SURE WHAT HE'S GOING TO DO. SUDDENLY HE PUTS HIS HAND UP HER DRESS. HE HOLDS HIS HAND THERE JUST FOR A MOMENT. SHE HOLDS VERY STILL, TENSE, THEN SLOWLY RISES ALMOST ON TIP TOE AS HE STARES INTO HER EYES.

VOICE (off): It's time.

JUST AS SUDDENLY BULL TAKES HIS HAND AWAY, AND BLONDE FALLS BACK DOWN, FLAT ON HER FEET. BULL TAKES A HANDKERCHIEF FROM HIS TOP POCKET AND DELIBERATELY WIPES HIS FINGER BEFORE PUTTING THE HANDKERCHIEF BACK IN PLACE.

BULL: Til we meet again.

AND HE'S GONE.

BLONDE: Give my love to your wife, baby!

THE DOOR SLAMS.

SHE SMOOTHES DOWN HER DRESS. SHE'S SHOCKED. SHE'S VERY AWARE OF BEING ALONE. SHE DOESN'T QUITE KNOW WHAT TO DO. SHE DOESN'T KNOW WHETHER TO CRY OR CELEBRATE. SHE PICKS UP THE EARRING BOX. A RECEIPT DROPS OUT. SHE READS IT.

BLONDE: 'With all good wishes from the President of Ghana.' Well, whaddya know?

SHE SITS ON THE BED, LOST AND ALONE. SHE TAKES A DRINK, WASHES IT DOWN WITH A PILL. SHE LIES ON THE BED, STARING AT THE CEILING.

2. THE OFFICE

A FEATURELESS OFFICE. THE SOUND OF AN OVERHEAD FAN. IT'S STILL TOO HOT. BULL'S FACED BY A YOUNGER MAN WHO IS THINNER, BUT ALSO GOOD LOOKING AND TANNED. HE'S TIGHTLY COILED, BUTTONED UP, THIN TIE, WIRY, MORE SERIOUS THAN THE ELDER MAN, LESS SELF ASSURED BUT NO LESS AMBITIOUS.

BEACH: Don't do this.

BULL DOESN'T SAY ANYTHING.

BEACH: Don't see her. Don't go near her. We need clear air here. Don't swim in murky water.
BULL: OK, quit now.

BULL DOESN'T SPEAK.

BEACH: She is not of sound mind. We know this. Take advice: they're all the same. Choose the one with the least baggage; she brings a whole carousel.

THE BULL APPRAISES HIM.

BULL: And this is your best advice?
BEACH: She wants something.
BULL: This girl has the world already -
BEACH: What'd she offer you?
BULL: Envy's a sin, boy.
BEACH: And your wife?
BULL: What did you say?

THIS STOPS BULL.

BULL: Who is what? To do with this? I don't hear her name here. Her name is not a part of this conversation.
BEACH: She will hear rumours.
BULL: From who? From you, you little fuck?
BEACH: Not from me –
BULL: You goddamn prick, if I find out it's you, I'll send you to run a cathouse in the Nevada desert!
BEACH: Hey, no! This is stupid -
BULL: Snitch!

BULL IS TEASING BUT, STILL, THIS ISN'T WORKING OUT HOW BEACH HOPED.

BEACH: Only you risk this being an open secret -
BULL: Then close it!
BEACH: You're not discreet.
BULL: I'm discreet.
BEACH: You go to see her. Who saw you go in? Who saw you come out? It's not like you're invisible, for Christ's sake.
BULL: So who saw me? No one.
BEACH: You go to the dentist too often.
BULL: So I'll go to the goddamn doctor!
BEACH: That's funny. But this is no joke. Rumours are rumours. Walls bleed secrets.
BULL: Goddammit, find out who's spreading these rumours, castrate the bastards, you got that?
BEACH: You can't do that to a girl.

THIS STOPS BULL.

BULL: You're saying it's her?

BEACH: She likes to drink.

BULL: She's saying these things?

BEACH: She's proud of her new conquest, why not tell folk the good news?

BULL: That's proof?! We have work to do.

BEACH: You get one of them pregnant -

BULL: Then we deny it!

FOR BULL, THE CONVERSATION IS NOW OVER.

BEACH: She can use you. She will if it suits. She likes attention. She's not stupid. She can do this: you make this possible.

BULL: You don't know her.

BEACH: And you do? You've seen inside her head? Listen, our people -

BULL: No, you listen! You have proof, I'll hear you out; you don't, give the poor girl a break, for Chrissakes!

BULL IS RIGHT IN HIS FACE.

BEACH: OK.

BULL: In my own time I do as I choose. This is understood?

BEACH: Don't let this get in the way of everything -

BULL: How? How does this one thing get in the way? This is nothing.

BEACH: You want me to tell you what she has for breakfast? What make of panty hose she wears? When she last shaved her legs, how many pounds she weighs, what pills she takes, how many abortions she's had -

BULL: OK!

BULL IS SILENT.

BEACH: This is not nothing. We are responsible people. An error doesn't become a mistake until we refuse to correct it.
BULL: And we will.
BEACH: No girl's worth so much.
BULL: Trust me, it's over.

BULL WALKS OUT.

3. THE BEDROOM

BULL'S DRESSING. IT'S BEEN A QUICK FUCK, NEITHER OF THEM HAS TAKEN MANY CLOTHES OFF.

BLONDE: Don't go. Baby, please. Stay awhile.

BUT HE'S GETTING READY TO LEAVE.

BLONDE: I bought you a toothbrush.
BULL: ?
BLONDE: Sure, I'm your dentist, remember, dummy.

HE LAUGHS. STARTS TO MOVE OFF THE BED. SHE PULLS HIM BACK DOWN.

BLONDE: Come back here, lover boy -
BULL: You're one crazy lady.
BLONDE: Hell, I'm way more crazy than that, baby, I'm crazy for /you -

SHE TRIES TO GRAB HIM AGAIN. HE FENDS HER OFF.

BULL: Quit that.
BLONDE: My mother ended up in an asylum, you know. Maybe, maybe I'll go to that place myself some day, won't I? If I get any crazier. What d'you think? Do you think I'm crazy?
BULL: I lost my tie.

HE'S PREOCCUPIED LOOKING FOR IT.

BLONDE: Baby?

BULL: No, you're not crazy.

BLONDE: Boy, if that were only true! If I could – if I could just believe that, well, maybe – well, maybe, wouldn't that be something! 'Cos sometimes I feel – sometimes I don't - I just – I feel like I'm breaking into a million and one tiny little pieces, and - and mother's there, well, of course she is, and - she's glowering at me!

BULL: I wish I could stay -

BLONDE: Then stay!

HE SAYS NOTHING.

BLONDE: You move too fast, life's all just a blur, isn't it, baby? You sure don't get to see the scenery!

BULL LOOKS AT HIS WATCH, GRIMACES IN APOLOGY, HEADS OFF TO THE BATHROOM TO LOOK FOR THE TIE.

BLONDE: Don't you like to hear me to talk?

BULL: Of course I do.

BLONDE: Sometimes I feel like my whole life's like - like it's – it's just rushing by, and I'm, I'm racing someplace but – but I'm – I'm going nowhere! There's no place else to go! And everyone's looking at me, but they don't see me. I'm invisible!

BULL: Let me tell you, you are far from invisible –

BLONDE: Well, sometimes a girl expects a little more from life than just waiting at the end of a phone line.

BLONDE GIVES BULL BACK HIS TIE - WHICH SHE HAS BEEN HIDING.

BULL: Didn't you like the necklace?
BLONDE: Which was probably just another present from the Emperor of India or someone. For your wife!
BULL: Is that what this is about?
BLONDE: No! No, baby, just shut me up. Tell me to stop talking, forget everything I say, won't you? I'm just feeling real sore today, baby. I'm blue. No. But, hey - hey! It's not about waiting for the storm to pass, it's about learning to dance in the rain, isn't it? Sure it is!

HE'S TIED HIS TIE, HE'S READY TO LEAVE.

BULL: OK.
BLONDE: Hey, you weren't even listening! You – you look like you're some other place already.

HE LOOKS AT HIS WATCH. THE MAN COMING FOR HIM IS LATE. HE MAKES A QUICK DECISION.

BULL: OK, I'll stay. Just for a short while.
BLONDE: OK? OK?? Now why didn't you say so earlier, dummy? Boy, we could have more fun! Wait, I'll fix you a drink.

SHE STARTS TO MAKE HIS DRINK: BOURBON ON THE ROCKS, AND ONE FOR HERSELF. SHE'S LIKE AN EXCITED CHILD.

BLONDE: Here – poison on the rocks. Only there ain't no rocks! And let's hope there ain't no poison neither!

HE DRINKS. SHE CLINKS GLASSES.

BLONDE: To us! Hey, you got a new watch!

BULL: A gift. From the Soviets.

BLONDE: Wow! You don't worry it's bugged? You ever think of that? Wouldn't that be just terrible! It'd be like – it'd be like that Trojan thing, that wooden horse!

BULL: Our people pulled it apart -

BLONDE: But if they were spying on you the whole time! I don't know how anyone could live like that! Poor baby. And what if - what if they really got to know what goes on in here, huh?

BULL: Which they won't.

BLONDE: But - what if they're listening right now? Or - or what if someone knows already? Oh no, that would be too awful –

BULL: My people swept the room. It's OK, it's clean.

BLONDE: Swept? Who? (She realises) For bugs! They did? Who did? When? You had people do it?

BULL: You're safe here.

BLONDE: People I don't know about? Were in this room? When I didn't give them a key.

BULL: They know what they're doing -

BLONDE: How'd they get in? Where did they look? Did they look through my drawers? What did they find?

BULL: They're gone now, forget it -

BLONDE: But what did they look at??

BULL: For Chrissakes, what did you expect!

HE CHECKS HIS WATCH.

BLONDE: I – I expect to be asked.

BULL: This is a precaution.

BLONDE: I expect to know.

BULL: To protect you. To help you. That's all we're trying to do.

BLONDE: Well, maybe I just need to know who's doing the

protecting.

BULL: They do a job.

BLONDE: You think that makes me feel safe? No! That makes me feel violated.

BULL: There's no violation.

BLONDE: That makes me feel like a prisoner! Sneaking around behind my back. Spying on me -

BULL: No one's spying on anybody! Honey, don't spoil this -

BLONDE: Why do you never use my name?

BULL: Why do you have to make this so goddamn hard?

BLONDE: I told you, maybe I'm just a little crazy today -

BULL: We had a nice time -

BLONDE: Oh yes, baby, we sure have fun, don't we?

BULL: You know what this is. This is what it is.

THE SILENCE HANGS HEAVY BETWEEN THEM.

BLONDE: I want to hear your voice in the morning. Rising from the first light of dawn. In the same room. In the same warm bed.

SILENCE.

BULL: You know that's impossible.

BLONDE: You make things possible.

BULL: Don't make this more than it is.

BLONDE: Oh, how mighty oaks fall.

BULL: I told you –

BLONDE: What if I tell the whole world you're my lover? How about if I tell them everything about us, Mr Presi/dent?

BULL: Goddammit!

HE SLAPS HER.

SILENCE.

BLONDE: You good old boys sure know how to treat a girl just right.
BULL: You don't tell anyone anything about what happens in this room. Ever.
BLONDE: Or what? What happens then, Mr Pres-i-dent? Or you're just afraid of making your pretty wife cry! Is that what this is? You think she doesn't know? From what I hear, she already has her own bedroom -

HE LIFTS HIS HAND AGAIN, BUT STOPS HIMSELF.

BLONDE: Go on, why don't you hit me again? Maybe this time I can stay face down on the carpet forever, oh wouldn't that be good? Peace at last! Baby, you haven't checked your watch in a while, maybe you do care about me - just a little! Or you're waiting for the man and the man don't come?

SHE SEES BY HIS REACTION THAT'S THE ANSWER.

BLONDE: So that's the way the cookie crumbles, huh?
BULL: This conversation never happened.
BLONDE: Sure it did. I have a real good memory.

SHE PUTS HER HAND TO HER FACE WHERE SHE WAS SLAPPED.

BLONDE: One night, is that really so much to ask?
BULL: I can stop this.
BLONDE: Oh yes, you're the power at the centre, aren't you? You're the Minotaur waiting in the maze.
BULL: What the hell are you talking about?

BLONDE: Boy, they all end in tragedy, don't they? You think those Greeks were ever happy? They sure don't sound like they had a whole lot of fun!

KNOCKING IS HEARD. THEY SPEAK QUIETLY.

BULL: What do you want?
BLONDE: I told you, baby.

ANOTHER KNOCK.

VOICE (off): Sir?
BLONDE: I want to wake beside you in the morning.

BULL SEEMS TO THINK FOR A MOMENT. THEN SUDDENLY:

BULL: That can't happen.

SUDDENLY, INCREDIBLY ABRUPTLY, BULL LEAVES, SLAMMING THE DOOR ON HIS WAY OUT. BLONDE'S LEFT CONFUSED AND BEREFT. SHE GRABS THE NEAREST GLASS.

BLONDE: Well, here's to you, darling! And all who sail in you!

SHE DRAINS THE LOT AND HEADS OFF FOR THE BATHROOM.

4. THE BEDROOM

BEACH IS IN THE BEDROOM, WAITING.

BLONDE COMES FROM THE BATHROOM, WEARING A BATH ROBE AND A TOWEL ROUND HER HEAD.

SHE'S SURPRISED TO SEE BEACH.

BLONDE: What - ?
BEACH: OK, ma'am.
BLONDE: What the hell are you doing here?
BEACH: OK, now.
BLONDE: *He* sent you.
BEACH: It's like this. I am here to tell you that he was never here. You have not met him -
BLONDE: Tell him he can come and disappoint me himself, he's a big bouncing boy.
BEACH: I'm sorry, the man is in no position to do that.
BLONDE: So I get to speak to the lucky – to the lackey.
BEACH: Are you drunk?
BLONDE: Can't a lady drink in her own home now or is that against the law or something? Hey, maybe you changed the law while I was showering, well of all the low down rotten dirty tricks - !
BEACH: How much have you drunk, ma'am?
BLONDE: And what kind of goddamn beeswax is that of yours, Mister?
BEACH: Then let me spell this out to you, once, clearly: there shall be no threat to the security of the United States.
BLONDE: I thought he hadn't met me.
BEACH: You will not call the Office. You will not divulge any conversations you may have had with the Office or the Office Holder -

BLONDE: My, he said you were one tight ass.

BEACH: You will not invent conversations you have or have not had with the Office or the Office Holder. You will not speak to any third party about said conversations, you will not circulate/ photographic material -

BEACH: Well, whoop-de-doo, and loop the frigging loop, well whaddya know? Say it ain' so, Joe!

SHE THINKS IT'S FUNNY. SHE GIGGLES.

BEACH: Ma'am, you need to pay attention here. Before this is out of control. Which you would not want to happen, to your own jeopardy.

SHE LAUGHS.

BLONDE: Don't you even speak English ever?

BEACH: Ma'am, the fun is over.

BLONDE: What am I, for Chrissakes? Scarlett fucking O'Hara?

BEACH: Ma'am, please -

BLONDE: Boy, I'm dangerous! Little old me! Well, ain't that a blast. A danger to the state. My mother sure would be proud of me! You want a drink?

BEACH: No!

BLONDE: Sure you do, beach boy, you're gasping.

SHE MAKES HIM ONE ANYWAY. HE'S NOT SURE HOW TO REACT.

BLONDE: Tell him to return my calls.

BEACH: Your calls are an embarrassment. They embarrass the girls on the switchboard. They embarrass you.

BLONDE: Are you queer?

BEACH: Ma'am –

BLONDE: You're all so scared of me, he sends his kid brother to wash his dirty linen in private?

BEACH: Ma'am, you need to understand where we are with this now.

BLONDE: You mean the fucking President no longer wants to fuck me.

BEACH: You need to keep your mouth closed, lady.

BLONDE: Except when I have to talk to him.

BEACH: That is no longer possible. /You need to cooperate here.

BLONDE: Heck, you're no more than a rinky dink skinny-ma-link beach boy.

SHE MOVES CLOSE, STARTS TO UNDO HIS TIE, BUTTONS. HE FIGHTS HER OFF.

BEACH: Stop that now.

BLONDE: Sure you're not just another sweet boy who wants something from me too, ain't you, baby?

BEACH: You need to understand this is in no way personal.

BLONDE: My, they sure coiled you fierce in the furnace!

BEACH: Lady, don't make me do anything which we might regret.

BLONDE: Wonder how you taste, boy.

FINALLY BEACH BREAKS FREE.

BEACH: Stop!

HE ALMOST THROWS HER AWAY. SHE TOTTERS, BUT JUST MANAGES NOT TO FALL. BEACH WIPES HIS FACE WITH A FASTIDIOUS LITTLE HANDKERCHIEF.

BLONDE: My, you smell like a prissy little church minister.
BEACH: You understand this is a situation not of our making, ma'am. The man -
BLONDE: Which man?
BEACH: He must be secure.
BLONDE: Well, not with all those atom bombs, he's not! No, siree, not when they're all aimed straight at him! He's the Minotaur in the maze! BOOM! And he's the one with his finger on the button!
BEACH: Stop this!

AN IMPASSE.

BEACH: You either help us or you're against us.
BLONDE: What if I'm just about lost - somewhere in the middle?

BEACH DOESN'T MOVE.

BLONDE: Why don't you come a little closer? Friends?

SHE LOOSENS HER BATHROBE. HE STAYS WHERE HE IS.

BLONDE: Everyone wants to look at me except you, now why is that?
BEACH: Forget it. We can tell people the way you are now. Look at this place! Who believes a drunk? It's over for you. Forget I was ever here. Forget you ever met him. OK? This is where it ends!
BLONDE: Tell him I want my child to have a father.

AS BEACH REALISES WHAT SHE MEANS IT IS LIKE

A PHYSICAL BLOW. HE TURNS ON HIS HEELS AND
HEADS OUT OF THE ROOM FAST.

5. THE BEDROOM

BLONDE IS ON THE PHONE.

BLONDE:

Then tell him it's Pussy Van Winkle!

That's right, you just tell him it's me.

Yes, I know he's busy, he's always busy. But he's expecting me to call -

No, *you* don't understand, this is real urgent, I need to talk to him right now!

Because I don't want to talk to no one else, do I? Not when it's him likes to hear my voice...

So maybe you don't know everything, do you, huh? You ever thought of that? Some things are secret even from you girls!

You wanna bet? Oh, boy, the things I could tell you, honey, they'll make your hair curl, you'd better believe it. So now, why don't you just put me through like a good girl -

I told you, I don't wanna talk to no one else, not when it's real personal!

Then where the hell is he? And what the hell happened to his old number, that's what I want to know. Did it die or something?

Well, if it's been reassigned, lady, then you just tell me what his new number is, why don't you, then I don't need to trouble you no more. Won't that make it easier for all of us?

Come on, you can tell me, I'm his friend, ain't I? He must've just forgot, 'cos I'm a real close personal friend. With news he *needs* to know. Now! And you're gonna be in real BIG trouble you don't let me speak to him, lady -

Oh go to hell, Miss Stuck Up Smarty Pants!

BLONDE GIVES UP, SLAMS THE PHONE DOWN.

6. THE BEDROOM

IT'S DARK. BLONDE'S TRYING TO SLEEP AND FAILING.

SHE'S AWARE THERE'S SOMEONE THERE IN THE DARK.

BULL: I'm not the one.
BLONDE: Who's that?
BULL: From what I hear.

SHE'S GRADUALLY COMING ROUND.

BLONDE: Deny it all you want, sugar.
BULL: I wasn't here. I've never been alone with you.
BLONDE: Well here's the thing, darling –
BULL: You're deluded. You make up stories, you're sick -
BLONDE: Sure, lover boy, that's me in a nutshell, what's your excuse?
BULL: You drink to excess. You have a known addiction to prescription drugs -
BLONDE: - of which club you're a member/ too, baby –
BULL: You have psychiatric problems. You want your whole life to be out there on the newsstands? You want your life to be over?
BLONDE: Au contraire, baby, I have all the life I need right here inside me.
BULL: That's simply not going to happen!
BLONDE: Wow, how manly you are in the dark! Now how are you going to stop me exactly? I want a child. My own child. I asked for one night. I wanted to tell you myself. One night, was that so high a price? Maybe I would even have got rid of her. For you. Who needs a child? I want my child

to have a father! Say something, baby.

SILENCE.

BLONDE: Is this where they come in? Where they put a bag over my head and throw me out with the trash, Mr President?
BULL: Quit using that name!
BLONDE: Imagine me an old lady, huh! Boy, it just doesn't bear thinking about, no, sir. I guess some of us just won't grow old gracefully, huh?

SHE TURNS ON THE LIGHT. SHE'S A MESS. HE'S SHOCKED.

BULL: Jeez!
BLONDE: I only wanted you to wake me in the morning, baby. We'd shoot the breeze, howl at the moon –
BULL: It's better like this, trust me -
BLONDE: Who for?
BULL: How could you bring a child into this world? Let's look at the truth here. I'm saying this as a friend. What kind of mother could you be?
BLONDE: Hey, I could be a fine mother if I set my mind to it! Stay with me.

SHE REACHES FOR HIM. HE RETREATS SO AS NOT TO BE TOUCHED.

BLONDE: You came to say goodbye.

HE DOESN'T ANSWER.

BLONDE: Maybe you're right, look at me, huh! White

trash, all washed up and no place to go. Baby, my brain hurts like a warehouse.

HE DOESN'T MOVE.

BLONDE: You didn't have to come back.

SHE PICKS UP A BOTTLE OF PILLS.

BULL: Hey! Stop.

SHE POPS TWO PILLS DELIBERATELY, THEN ONE MORE FOR LUCK, SWIGS THEM DOWN WITH A GLASS OF DRINK BESIDE HER.

BLONDE: It's not my fault, I'm a light sleeper!
BULL: What are those?
BLONDE: How should I know, sugar, I just take 'em! One, two, three and down the hatch, baby!

HE STOPS HER TAKING ANY MORE, TAKES THE BOTTLE FROM HER.

BULL: Don't take any more.
BLONDE: What's it to you, anyways? I never met you before, you don't know me! "He was never here, your honour, I swear!" Oh, quit gawping like some dumb fish.
BULL: You want people to see you like this?
BLONDE: Oh, you just want me sober and boring and ugly. Like a – a – like a barefoot housewife!

SHE STARTS TO GET UP, SHE'S PRETTY UNSTEADY.

BULL: You need to get cleaned up. You need to get this place cleaned up.

BLONDE: Sure I do.

SHE FALLS.

BLONDE: Oh, shit-fuckers!
BULL: Here –
BLONDE: Whoops! Well and that sure weren't very
ladylike, was it, pardon my French. Takes so many drinks
just to stand straight. Like, like the sea came into the room
and washed away all the parts of me that meant anything.
BULL: So quit drinking.
BLONDE: Oh don't be such a kill-joy! If I don't drink then
what happens to all the poor liquor companies, you tell me
that, huh? They don't get rich, that's for sure! And then the
poor government doesn't get any taxes. It's my patriotic
duty! Who are you?
BULL: What?
BLONDE: I've seen you before, haven't I? You're someone
special.
BULL: No more games now -
BLONDE: Hey, I know you, don't I? You're the one won't
stay the night, you never stay over, why not, sailor? Because
you're married! BULLS-EYE! Because because - Because
you don't love me! Because you're a coward without a bone
brave enough in your body to - to do what you really want to
do, what you really want to do it, don't you?

SHE'S NOT MAKING A LOT OF SENSE:

BULL: You don't know what I want.
BLONDE: Oh, you're boring, you sound like the other one.
Listen. Listen, listen - How'd you like one last tumble in the
hay, Mr President, for good old lay - lady America! Boy,
how'd you like them apples? Remember the good times,

baby! They sure were fun! (sings) I wanna be loved by you and nobody else but you -

SHE LAUGHS RAUCOUSLY, CLIMBS UP ON THE BED, LIFTS HER NIGHTDRESS TO SHOW A LEG, SLINKS ONE STRAP DOWN OVER HER SHOULDER, BLAZES WITH LIFE.

BLONDE: Come and get it baby, the last chance saloon is open and I'm ready to drink this town dry!

SHE REACHES OUT TO HIM. BUT IT'S CLEAR HE'S NOT BUYING.

BLONDE: No?
BULL: No.
BLONDE: Oh, why don't you just send over your goddamn spooks to come clean up here? Sure. Clean me up and clean me out while you're all about it? I was beautiful, wasn't I? Only now. Now - Don't look at me like that, baby, I disgust you, jeez, what the hell's wrong with me!? Ugly, you're ugly, that's you, close the shutters, turn off the light, you're not perfect, you're far from perfect. Hell-fire, turn off the damn light!

IN RISING PANIC, SHE STARTS HITTING HER FACE. HE TRIES TO STOP HER, BUT SHE'S FEROCIOUS.

BLONDE: Useless, useless, useless –
BULL: Hey! Quit!
BLONDE: No one wants you, no one wants you, white trash,/ get used to it, no one wants –
BULL: Everyone wants you.
BLONDE: LIAR!

BULL: Shhh!

FINALLY HE MANAGES TO GET HER HANDS SO SHE CAN'T HIT HERSELF. SHE'S QUIET.

BLONDE: Imagine me married to the President, huh? Boy, that'd sure be something, wouldn't it? Then I'd be somebody! Then they wouldn't be able to make fun of me no more, would they? Am I beautiful?
BULL: Yes. Yes, you are.
BLONDE: Honest injun?
BULL: That's the truth.
BLONDE: The whole truth? Jeez! So beautiful you could die?
BULL: And go to heaven too.
BLONDE: Wowza! That's a compliment! From the big cheese himself! *And* I'm smart! Baby, you look real sad. Like a bull ready for the slaughterhouse. Tick, tock, tick, tock, got your finger on the button. Murderer.
BULL: Shhh -

SUDDENLY SHE TURNS ON HIM, FIERCE.

BLONDE: Goddamn lying murderer!

SHE ATTACKS HIM, TRYING TO CLAW, RIP AND PULL ANYTHING SHE CAN GET HER HANDS ON.

BLONDE: Murderer! Murderer!

HE LEAPS AWAY TO ESCAPE. SHE FLAILS AFTER HIM, LEAPS ON HIS BACK. IT HURTS. IT'S MESSY. SUDDENLY SHE'S BEGGING:

BLONDE: Oh baby, stay with me, please, please, please, please, stay with me, stay with me, don't leave, baby, stay with me, stay - !
BULL: Get the hell off me!

BEACH COMES IN THE DOOR.

BEACH: Jesus!
BLONDE: Well, hello there, cutie. You wanna join us?
BEACH: OK, OK, you're right out of here right now!
BLONDE: Hey, we're busy! Wrestling alligators in the swamp of American dreams!

BULL TRIES TO GET UP, BUT SHE HOLDS TIGHT, PULLS HIM DOWN.

BEACH: Christ!
BULL: Let me go -

BEACH STARTS TRYING TO PULL HER OFF. BULL FINALLY ESCAPES.

BLONDE: Go then, run! See for all I care! You won't get far!
BEACH: I told you this!
BLONDE: You wanna get laid too, beach boy?

SUDDENLY BLONDE GRABS BEACH. HE STRUGGLES TO GET AWAY, BUT CAN'T ESCAPE.

BULL: Christ!
BEACH: You need serious help, lady.
BLONDE: Sure, lower your blood pressure 'fore your teeth explode!

BEACH: We shouldn't be here, we agreed this -
BLONDE: (to Bull) And I thought you were the boss, sailor!
BEACH: We're out of here.

BEACH FINALLY MANAGES TO GET AWAY FROM BLONDE. BEACH AND BULL ESCAPE TO THE DOOR.

BLONDE: Happy birthday to you.

SHE SINGS. IT'S FILTHY AND SEXY, ONE LAST BURST OF GLORY. THEY WATCH, HORRIFIED, ATTRACTED DESPITE EVERYTHING.

BLONDE: Happy birthday to you.
Happy birthday, dear what's your name -

SHE'S HEADING FOR BULL.

BLONDE: Happy birthday - fuck you.

SHE TURNS FROM BULL AND SUDDENLY KISSES BEACH FULL ON THE LIPS. BEACH PULLS AWAY. BULL SEES BEACH'S CONFUSION, REALISES SOMETHING. LOOKS AT BEACH, THUNDEROUS.

BLONDE: That's right, baby, you were busy, always so busy.
BEACH: I don't know what this even is.
BLONDE: Oh, he woke me in the morning with coffee and waffles. Such a gentleman.
BEACH: This is not something that happened!
BLONDE: No wham bam thank you ma'am, no sir, this one loved me the whole night through! A woman just doesn't

like to feel invisible. She wants someone who actually gives a damn! He woke me in the morning with a kiss gentle as a butterfly's wing, whispered soft as a rose, kissed me over and over like a lover should. You never kissed me. Not once.
BULL: Maybe I hated the idea of so many mouths before me.

BEACH GRABS BULL.

BEACH: This is over.
BULL: Get your goddamn hands off me!

BULL PULLS AWAY FROM BEACH. BEACH RETREATS TO THE DOORWAY BUT WAITS. BULL FACES BLONDE.

BULL: It's not his goddamn birthday.

THEN THE MEN ARE GONE.

BLONDE IS LEFT ALL ALONE.

SHE GOES FOR THE PILLS.

7. THE BEDROOM

BLONDE'S IN BED, TRYING TO SLEEP. IN THE DARK, SHE HEARS SOMETHING.

BLONDE: Who's that?

SILENCE.

BLONDE: You can't fool me, I heard you, I know you're there!

SILENCE.

BLONDE: I'll call the cops. Yes, I will. They love me!

SHE THINKS IT'S BULL.

BLONDE: Hey, I didn't mean it. I just said those things! Just to make you pay attention. I need – I need to see you. Just for one goddamned night, is that too much to ask!? We could get married, maybe we could have children, we could have a child maybe, we could run away some place -

BUT THERE'S NO ONE THERE.

BLONDE: Where are you?

SHE'S IMAGINED IT. SHE TAKES A FISTFUL OF PILLS AND WASHES THEM DOWN WITH BOURBON.

BLONDE: Bottoms up and down the hatch, that oughta hit the spot, sailor!

HER STOMACH HURTS. BLONDE HEARS A NOISE.

BLONDE: Hey, is that you? You there, baby?

SOMEWHERE A DOOR SLAMS.

BLONDE: Baby?

SILENCE.

ANOTHER DOOR IS HEARD.

BLONDE: Baby, you came back!

THERE'S NO ONE THERE.

BLONDE: Where are you, baby? You hiding? You want a chase, is that it? Well, then I'm a coming to get you, big bad wolf!

SHE DRINKS AND TAKES MORE PILLS.

BLONDE: You all want a piece of me, but you sure don't want the whole of me, do you? Well, how'd you like them apples!

SHE LOOKS AT THE PILLS CONFUSED, NOT SURE HOW MANY SHE'S TAKEN, TAKES MORE ANYWAY. HER STOMACH HURTS. SHE SINKS ON THE BED. SHE LOOKS ROUND, DOESN'T SEEM TO KNOW WHERE SHE IS. SHE WANTS TO GET UP, FINDS SHE CAN'T. SHE'S SLURRING HER WORDS. SHE TRIES HARDER. SHE TRIES TO MAKE A CALL, BUT CAN'T WORK OUT THE NUMBERS.

BLONDE: I need to – I need to speak to the Pres- the President of the US of A -

THE PHONE FALLS OUT OF HER HAND. SHE SLUMPS BACK ON THE BED. SHE CALLS QUIETLY LIKE A WOUNDED, DYING ANIMAL.

BLONDE: Help me! Someone, please help!

SILENCE.

SHE TRIES TO GET OUT OF THE BED. SHE DOESN'T MAKE IT, BUT ENDS UP SLUMPED HALF IN AND HALF OUT OF THE COVERS.

8. THE BEDROOM/OFFICE

BULL AND BEACH IN THE OFFICE/AT THE SAME TIME, BLONDE, UNMOVING, IN THE BEDROOM.

BULL: This is a mess. A goddamn mess! What the hell happened?
BEACH: I warned you -
BULL: In no way am I associated with this -
BEACH: The place will be deep cleaned -
BULL: This thing gives me a headache.
BEACH: Don't worry, you'll lead a long, happy life.

BULL MASSAGES HIS HEAD. HE GRUNTS IN PAIN.

BULL: Why the deep clean?
BEACH: Trust me, you don't want to know.
BULL: What is it I do not need to know?
BEACH: OK.

BEAT.

BEACH: There's a microphone behind the radiator, a wiretap on the telephone, a mike behind the headboard of the bed -
BULL: Uh-huh -
BEACH: - one above the big picture, one above the front door, another in the green vase, a camera in the bedroom fan, a mike in the bathroom-
BULL: Whoa, whoa, who said anything about a camera? In the goddamn bedroom? Who put a fucking camera in there, who is this creep?
BEACH: The camera guy.
BULL: Well, you tell this creep he can pack his bags and

head for - I mean, the silly bastard! - Alaska! – Jesus! And leave the nosy, snooping bastard there for the rest of his natural goddamn fucking life, you hear me?!

BEACH: He's the one called us.

BULL: He called us?

BEACH: He was on duty.

BULL: And so he called us?

BEACH: He called us first. Trust me, without him, this is a problem –

BULL: Jeez -

BULL'S HEAD HURTS. BEACH REACHES OUT TO HIM.

BEACH: You're OK?

BULL: I need a girl.

BEACH: She's barely cold!

BULL: And I need to warm my bones! It's over, forget it. Shit happens.

BEACH: She deserves more. Doesn't she?

BULL: You fuck her, little brother? She was telling the truth?

BEACH: You think she knew what the truth was.

BULL: Christ, this is not our fault! This is a whole life messed up before we even laid eyes on her.

BEACH DOESN'T WANT TO HEAR IT.

BULL: You reach as high as you can, you're lucky you don't get burned.

NO ANSWER.

BULL: Hey! This is what it is. You think I'm an animal?

BEACH DOESN'T RESPOND.

BULL: There will be no record. No private souvenirs, no mementoes. Nothing is talked about. Nothing gets so much as a historical footnote.

BEACH STILL DOESN'T SPEAK.

BULL: The lady was unhappy. She had a dying wish. She checked out early. We have work to do.

BULL LEAVES. BEACH IS LEFT ALONE.

9. THE BEDROOM

BEACH, AT THE DOOR, SEES THE DEAD BLONDE. HE CHECKS THE BEDROOM. COVERS THE CAMERA. FINDS A SINGLE GLASS ON THE FLOOR, FINDS THE EARRING BOX WITH ONE EARRING. GOES INTO THE BATHROOM, WHERE HE FINDS A PEARL NECKLACE. HE FINDS A NOTEBOOK/DIARY ON THE SIDE TABLE. HE'S ABOUT TO LEAVE WHEN HE STOPS. HE LOOKS AT THE BODY. BLONDE'S LYING ACROSS THE BED. SHE'S BEAUTIFUL EVEN IN DEATH.

HE TURNS HER OVER ON HER BACK. ONE LAST LOOK.

HE MOVES CLOSER, BREATHES CLOSE TO HER FACE, DRAWS HER SMELL IN CLOSE TO HIM. HE KISSES HER CHEEK. THEN HER COLD LIPS.

THEN HER NECK AND BREASTS.

HE PULLS BACK, LOOKS AT HER BODY. HE STARTS TO LIFT THE HEM OF HER SKIRT. HE SHIFTS TO GET MORE COMFORTABLE. HE LOOKS AROUND NERVOUSLY. HE STARES AT HER. HE CROUCHES BETWEEN HER KNEES, STARTS TO MOVE THEM APART. HE STARTS TO UNDO HIS TROUSERS.

JUST IN TIME HE REALISES WHAT HE'S DOING.

BEACH: Jesus! Fuck! Fuck, fuck, fuck –

HE SHOOTS OFF THE BED, DOES HIS TROUSERS UP,

HE CAN'T BELIEVE WHAT HE'S NEARLY DONE. HE'S SHAKING.

HE CAN'T THINK STRAIGHT, HE PULLS HIMSELF TOGETHER. HE LOOKS AROUND.

BEACH: OK, OK -

AT THE LAST MINUTE HE SEES SOMETHING.

HE REMOVES A FINAL EARRING FROM BLONDE, ONE OF THE PAIR THAT BULL GAVE HER. HE POCKETS THEM, AND HEADS FOR THE DOOR.

HE OPENS THE DOOR.

BEACH: OK, get her ready.

AND HE'S GONE.

ENDS.

WAKE ME IN THE MORNING

ALSO BY JEREMY RAISON

BRING ME SUNSHINE
Four actors (2m, 2f)
Eric isn't feeling well and feels worse when he realises Ernie is doing a funeral oration for him. Carol just wants her husband back, but something terrible has happened. Angie tries to help. A moving comedy, featuring two men who may or may not be Eric Morecambe and Ernie Wise.

THE RAIN GATHERING
Two actors (1m, 1f)
A twenty something couple at the tail end of their relationship reveal their story in flashbacks. This award-winning play was a big hit when first performed at the National and Traverse Theatres and on BBC Radio 4.

THERESE RAQUIN
Five actors, (3m, 2f), optional chorus
Zola's classic tale given thrillingly theatrical treatment in an acclaimed version for Glasgow Citizens Theatre. Therese is already married to her sickly cousin, Camille, when worldly Laurent is invited into her home. Murder brings Laurent and Therese together.

CANDYLAND
Three actors (2m, 1f)
Star has retreated to an aircraft hangar in the Nevada desert to live in peaceful seclusion with the woman he loves. Then City turns up uninvited. Soon it becomes clear that Star's idyllic isolation is not all it seems.

THE SOUND OF MY VOICE
Two actors (1m, 1f)
Morris Magellan is a successful executive. He is also a chronic alcoholic. Classic Ron Butlin adapted with great success for the Citizens Theatre, receiving 4 awards and seven 5 star reviews.

HEART AND SOUL
Seven actor/musicians (4m, 3f)
Old school-friends reform their band for a wedding, but they've changed and life isn't easy. Then the last member of the band arrives, a huge success in her musical career, and events spin out of control.